BY STRANGE PATHS

An Autobiography

by a Benedictine of Kylemore Abbey

Dame Elizabeth M. Magdalen Lee, O.S.B.

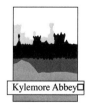

Kylemore Abbey

Kylemore Abbey Publications
Kylemore Abbey
Connemara
Co Galway

First published in 2002 by
Kylemore Abbey Publications
Kylemore Abbey
Connemara
Co Galway
telephone: 00 353 (0) 95 41146
email: info@kylemoreabbey.ie
www.kylemoreabbey.com

ISBN Number 0-9542310-0-7

Edited by Kathleen Villiers-Tuthill
Printed by ColourBooks Ltd
Design and layout by Bernard Kaye
Cover image from Kylemore Abbey private collection

BY STRANGE PATHS

Foreword

Mother Abbess Magdalena FitzGibbon, O.S.B.

Dame Elizabeth M. Magdalen Lee was a member of the Benedictine Community at Kylemore Abbey from 1919 until her death on 14 March 1952. Born in England she was brought up in the Protestant Faith and was received into the Roman Catholic Church at Lierre (Lier), Belgium, while studying there as a mature student, in 1898. A year later she entered the Ursuline Convent in Lierre and was professed in 1900. At the outbreak of the first World War in 1914, she, along with the rest of her Community, sought refuge at St. Mary's Priory, Princethorpe, England. At Princethorpe, she came in contact with the Benedictine tradition of *Opus Dei* and the plainchant and, as she herself explains: 'An overwhelming conviction came to me that this monastic life was the life I had longed for. From the depths of my soul came the cry: - O God let this life be mine; let me live and die here'.

Recognizing this as her true calling, she requested permission to join a Benedictine community. Our Community, themselves having been forced to abandon their convent at Ypres, Belgium, was, at the time, attempting to establish a convent and school at Macmine Castle in Co Wexford.

She came to Macmine in 1918 and became a Benedictine nun on 21 March 1919. Dr. Codd, Bishop of Ferns, officiated at the ceremony and Blessed Dom Columba Marmion, who had taken an interest in her progress, was among those present.

By Strange Paths tells of her search for God and for a suitable religious community to help her live out her particular calling. Dame Magdalen was obviously a woman of great faith and we are pleased to publish her story, as told here in her very own personal style.

M. Magdalena fitzGibbon OSB

Dame Elizabeth M. Magdalen Lee O.S.B.
(1875 - 1952)

"O God let this life be mine; let me live and die here"

A WORD OF EXPLANATION

The very few people who drew this story from me begged me to write it. I refused for several reasons, one of them being my conviction that only those who will know me could be interested in it.

Another reason was my inability to see what I write. Some twenty years ago, an incurable disease in the vital part of both eyes deprived me of most of my sight. Though a blessing in disguise, this has been a calamity (humanly speaking) for I cannot read a word, and, when I write, I only see, dimly, black lines on white paper. Consequently, it is extremely difficult to write coherently. My brain travels more quickly than my pen, and then, by the time I have reached the end of the sentence, I have forgotten the beginning of it, and have probably left the poor subject floating in the air, without its verb to support it.

But when suddenly it occurred to me that it might be ungrateful on my part to leave God's wonderful mercies unrecorded, I relented and attempted the impossible. Here it is. Please be indulgent!

I should like to thank my kind little friend, B.N.B. for reading it aloud to me, and supplying missing words which my tricky pen had omitted.

Perhaps this may fall into the hands of some who are stricken with anguish of soul, and it may help them to rest in the Lord, to wait patiently for him, till He give them their heart's desire.

> Kylemore Abbey.
> February 8th, 1945
> my 70th birthday.

Dame Magdalen and the Benedictine Community with The Most Rev. Dr. Walsh, Archbishop of Tuam, on the occasion of Lady Abbess Placid's Golden Jubilee in 1946.

Chapter 1

Few children, I think, loved school as I did. Even as a small child, all my interests were centred in it, and when at the age of thirteen I was sent to a larger and far better school, my delight was unbounded. School life then meant everything to me. All else was eclipsed by it, even the joys and interests of home. When evening came, I longed for dawn that I might return to the society of loved companions, whose affection gilded my life. I was up with the lark, singing as I dressed, snatches of the really beautiful songs we learned at school.

Heigh he for merry June,
Heigh, ho heigh!
All the earth is then a tune
Heigh, ho heigh!

Mine was, certainly. Then there was: -

In the evening to sweet music
We will dance upon the green.
O were e'er such happy mortals
Ever seen, ever seen.

I sang too as I walked briskly down the lovely country lane, which was a short cut to my school. Only in stormy weather, when the mill stream would be flooded, I had to go through the town and the merry songs had to be hushed.

But the great attraction was not merely the society of charming friends of my own age, it was the magnetic personality of our Head Mistress, Miss E.A. Bebbington. She had come to us straight from Newnham College, Cambridge, where she had gained her History Tripos, and in her were embodied the high and lofty principles of women like Helen Gladstone (The President) and other noble lights of the educational world. She radiated all that was noble, pure and beautiful. Words fail me in attempting to describe the greatness of her influence. Suffice it to say she became, as it were, and guiding star of my life, and to her I owe everything.

I was not the only one to be drawn by this magnet. All my friends were drawn in the same way, and this love for our Head was the strongest bond in our friendship. To this day, I am amazed at our girlish efforts to reproduce in our lives, the pure and lofty principles she so quietly and unostentatiously held before us. Only the best books would we read, hear the best music, and exclude from our conversation any word or any topic of which she would not approve. She was moreover, a deeply religious woman, of the High Anglican type, but she lived her religion rather than preached it. Therein lay the secret of her power. She arranged for Confirmation classes to be held at school, and I think that on that June day, so solemn to each member of our little group, there were no others in the land more ardent than we were. To our Head it was a deep joy to see the first fruits of her labour of love. She was supremely happy in the knowledge that to her it was given to mould our young lives. She was in her element, and I have always thought that these three or four years were the happiest of her life. To me, their joy was intoxicating. Moreover, success had come to me in my studies, and to me fell the coveted honour of being head of the school.

That marked the height of my happiness. Then the blow fell, and my fool's paradise with it. Miss Bebbington came back after the holidays wearing a diamond ring on the engagement finger. Diamonds cut, and her diamond cut deeply into my girlish soul. It cut away all the moorings which had held me spell-bound in a world of amorous romance, and cast me adrift into a world of prosaic realities. Well for me that it did so! Miss Bebbington resigned and was married that same year.

I stayed with her twice in her new home. Each time the impression left on me was this:- 'You are not as happy as you were formerly; if that is married life, no, thank you.'

Without her, school was a lonely desert, and I suffered unspeakably, but studies had to go on, and exams had to be passed. Gradually, and very dimly at first, I began to realise, to perceive the harmful influence wrought upon me by those years of infatuation, in spite of the very definite and very real ennobling influence that had been at work, yet at the same time my life had been altogether unbalanced. School life had become all in all, home life, nothing. Home was just a place in which to sleep and take one's meals.

My dear mother saw the change that had come over me, and grieved at it. She was naturally jealous of the intruder who had stolen the affection once given to herself. I cared nothing for the society of my sister, who was nearly two years younger than I. Unless forced, I would not go out with her. 'She doesn't know how to behave,' was my excuse, and 'she always comes to pieces on the way. Her stockings come down, or her shoe lace breaks, or one of her garments loses a button and drops down. I am ashamed to be seen with her.' Much of this was true, for my sister did not care a jot about her appearance, and hated to meet my 'grand friends' as she called them. For my brother, who was seven years my senior, I had the greatest admiration, a sort of hero worship, but he was not at home.

Blows rarely come alone. It was so with me, for some two months after the marriage of Miss Bebbington, came the most terrible blow of my life. My mother died. I was not quite seventeen, but this blow changed girlhood into premature womanhood. The sting of remorse was unspeakably sharp. It entered into every fibre of my being, and changed the whole of my life. If only she could have lived a few years longer. I might have regained my balance and might have been the comfort to her that I had been in earlier days. But to lose her in the midst of this estrangement! It was unbearable.

Strangely enough, it was my once-despised sister who saved me from despair. She had not been at home during mother's short illness, and only arrived after her death. I was so absorbed in my own misery that I hardly thought of my poor little sister. What she said was so simple and so natural, that it is difficult to explain to others the tremendous effect her words had upon me. 'Did mother leave no message for me?' was all she said. Her question startled me at first, for there had been no message, as mother had been unconscious. As I suddenly realised what this must mean to my little sister, some immense force of pity pierced my heart, until than so callous, but never callous again. It was as if the floodgates of a mighty love, dormant until then, had been forced open, filling me with a strong, deep, almost mother-like love for the sister who, until then, had been nothing but a nuisance, if not a nonentity. That love has never waned. Throughout the rest of her girlhood and her womanhood I have always mothered her, and am doing so still.

I loved my father tenderly, and always avoided doing or saying anything that could pain him, but at seventeen I was too inexperienced and, alas!, too self centred to fill my mother's place in his regard. The housekeeper was efficient, though extravagant, I was absorbed in my studies, and thought all was going well, in spite of my own personal misery and remorse, so the news of his approaching marriage came as a sudden blow. But I was already so dejected that nothing seemed to matter and I cannot now remember who told me, probably the housekeeper. My father would have been too shy and reticent to break such news to me, but I remember distinctly the evening when he told me he was bringing a lady to tea, and he knew I should welcome her and have everything as nice as possible. I did so, and made things as easy for him as I could, and never did I let him see any sign of disapproval or resentment. When asked to accompany them on a visit to her home some twenty miles away, I did so at once. I felt as if I were on the stage, acting a part.

The marriage eventually took place, and 'Ma', as we agreed to call her, took her place at my father's side. By this time, I was the only one at home. My sister often came home at weekends and my brother, who lived a few miles away, regularly called in. My sister had a sweet and easy, happy-go-lucky temperament, and immediately adapted herself to the change. I tried exceedingly hard to do so, for my dear father's sake.

The Sundays that brought my sister home were indeed warm days in my chilled life. We spent the greater part of the day together, and invariably went to church morning and evening, as we were both ardent Anglicans. My sorrows had thrown me back upon God, and now religion was a reality to me. I found solace in the beautiful services of the church, and always came away strengthened and comforted. My brother's visits were a joy too, and a stroll with him through our beautiful parks - Richmond Park, Home and Bushy Park, with an occasional visit to a La Crosse or Football match, were always refreshing and a relief from the tension at home.

Try as I would, I could not get on with Ma. In spite of all my care, I was always putting my foot in it. My brother said nothing. I think his sympathy was with me, but he was gentle and timid and anxious to remain neutral. For about two years I did my utmost to endure the constant friction, but one evening matters came to a climax over some paltry little incident which I have forgotten, and there was a scene. I was quite calm, yet desperate. I said, 'I can bear this no longer. I'll walk the streets rather than sleep another night in this house.' My father was too overcome to say a word. I can remember slipping off my shoes, and putting on my boots, coat and hat. I probably kissed my father goodbye, and out into the night I went. I was boiling with anger and indignation, and needed the cool night air to calm the throbbing pulse.

I did not walk the streets, but went to the house of a dear old friend of my mother's who was startled by my appearance at so late an hour. She and her husband were all sympathy. Neither of them could bear my stepmother. At once they began making arrangements to put me up for the night. A knock sounded at the door. It was my dear father. 'Come home with me', he said, very quietly, 'I will make things all right.' He was always a man of few words.

I flung my arms round him and said, 'For your sake, I will', and I went with him arm in arm. I do not remember what happened when I reached home, perhaps Ma had gone to her room. But I do remember telling my brother the whole story next day, and he insisted I should leave home at once, amicably of course, for father's sake.

He was most sympathetic and went at once to the house of my greatest friend, Mary Timson, and asked her mother, who was a widow, if she would receive me as a paying guest. No words could adequately describe my relief and my gratitude when she agreed. To live side by side in the sweet companionship of such a friend as Mary was heaven on earth after the misery I had endured. Her mother was so kind, treating me as her daughter.

By this time I was twenty. I had successfully passed the Higher Local Exams in Mathematics, French, German and History, gaining Honours in the last three, and in those days that certificate qualified me to teach in any High School. Mary was qualifying for Music, and we were both junior Mistresses in our dear old school, which we still loved and cherished. So we walked to school together, dined together, played and sang together in the evenings and went to church together. It was a delightful experience for both of us; for her, because she had no sister and only one younger brother, and for me, in my loneliness. I used to see my father quite often. He was always pleased to see me, but I think he, too, was really relieved that the friction had come to an end.

Among the group of school friends I mentioned at the beginning of my story was one named Sallie Barnard. She was charming, fascinating and most original. She had spent some years of her childhood at school in Germany, and when I used to go and stay with her, she would read her German diary to me, and tell me all about her school days. This had fired me with a secret desire to go to school in Germany some day. My brother tried to dissuade me, but in vain. The idea always rested at the back of my mind, to be realized at some future date. I had a decided taste for modern languages. I had studied them carefully, but I could not speak them fluently. Supposing I went to Germany, and later to France, in order to make myself truly proficient in both languages, and then I might be able to get my degree in modern languages?

This would give me a status in the educational world. The idea grew upon me and gradually took form, and eventually I obtained a post at a school in Görlitz, (Silesia). There I was to teach a couple of hours daily and do some supervision, in return for which I might attend any of the lectures given in the school, and also receive a small salary. The latter was no more than pocket money, but it sufficed to pay for stamps and small incidental expenses.

The natural excitement of getting new clothes for the new venture, and of making other preparations, was so absorbing that I hardly realised how terribly hard the parting with brother and sister and friend was going to be. I shall never forget that terrible wrench when it came. My brother did everything for me, and even took me to London to see me off in the boat train. I was just twenty-one, quite young for those days to undertake such a journey into an unknown world. But it was the realisation of a dream, and I was buoyed up by the anticipation of a new life. Suddenly, as we two stood on the cold platform waiting for the boat train, without any warning, I began to feel a horrible sinking sort of feeling. Tears rushed to my eyes and began to stream down my cheeks. I was amazed, so was my brother, and I was horribly ashamed of being such a baby. I stammered out, 'I'm not crying, I'm quite happy and I want to go.' He put his arm around me. I brushed away the tears. The train steamed in, and smiling through the tears which persisted in coming. I said goodbye, assured him again that I was quite happy, and that this was some silly nonsense that had come upon me. Then I was off: with Mary's voice still ringing in my ears, as she sang my favourite song; - 'God keep you ever His sunlight to feel' (Solveig's song).

Chapter 2

It was an April morning in 1896. The crossing was a pleasant one, and I was soon speeding through watery Holland into Germany. All that day I travelled, and all night, arriving in Dresden about noon the following day. I was to stay a few days there before continuing my journey to Görlitz Never before had I been abroad, so everything was novel to me. Eyes and ears were unable to take in all I saw and heard.

A gentleman and his wife, who were staying at the boarding house, had taken tickets for *Lohengrin* at the Royal Opera House, and I went with the rest of the party. To say that I was stunned by the magnificence around me would be only half the truth. I had not even been to one of our great London theatres, but only to the smaller provincial ones, so this superb Opera House was the revelation of a world unknown to me, and I was spell-bound. We were in the dress circle. I was surrounded by beautifully dressed ladies, and brilliantly decked-out officers. So many uniforms at first puzzled me, then I remembered that German officers are always obliged to be in uniform. The plan itself was entrancing. After all these years, I can still see Elsa, looking the embodiment of beauty and purity, as she stood there in her soft white gown, and the knightly Lohengrin in shining armour, singing his swan song.

After this excitement, following immediately the excitement of the goodbyes at home and the long journey, it was no wonder that I slept on and on far into the next day. Soon uneasiness was felt lest I should be ill, and a maid was at last sent into my room to see what had happened!

I saw the sights of Dresden, and spent much time in the beautiful picture galleries. My favourite picture was, of course, the *Madonna Sistina*, in a room all to itself. A small bench was placed opposite the famous picture, and there visitors sat and gazed and gazed. Thanks to the artistic training my dear brother had given me, I was able to appreciate a good picture. It was the expression in the face of the Christ-child that held my attention. There was almost pain in the exquisite little mouth, slightly drawn at the corners, and in the wide-opened eyes. There was mystery; the mystery of the Incarnation and the Redemption. I can still see it as I saw it then, and it is a lovely memory.

On the Sunday I spent in Dresden, the house party proposed to take a trip down the Elbe to a lovely spot known as the 'Switzerland of Saxony'. I longed to accept the invitation given me to join the party, but my conscience became uneasy for this reason. In Dresden there was an English Church, where I could receive Holy Communion, while in Görlitz there would be none. This was my last chance, and it seemed my duty to take it. I did so, and God rewarded this sacrifice in later years. I just mention this, because I think such little events become milestones along life's way.

The next day I arrived at my destination, the town of Görlitz, prettily situated on the river Neisse, in sight of the distant Riesengebirge or Giant-Mountains. I was surprised by the warm welcome given me by the Lady Principal. I suppose I looked very young and girlish; in any case, she put both arms round me and kissed me, inquiring in a most motherly way about my journey: 'You must be very tired, we are just going to have afternoon coffee, so come and have some with us.' I followed her and her two sisters into a long dining room, and we sat at the end of a very long table. It was quite an informal meal, if meal it could be called. On the table stood a large sort of coffee peculator with a lamp under it, a butter dish, and a plate with some queer looking things on it, about the size of a tea plate. I took one and seeing that they buttered theirs, I buttered mine, broke it up, as they did, (it was too brittle to cut) and discovered it was a delicious vanilla flavoured wafer. 'You must have an egg after your long journey', they said, and lo and behold, an egg was dropped into the top part of the strange sort of coffee percolator and lamp, and presently taken out with a spoon and presented to me. I was much amused at this procedure, but of course, showed none of my feelings. I did not like to ask for bread and butter and salt, but made a brave attempt to eat the egg with my Vanilla wafer, and succeeded, thanks to the good coffee which washed down the unusual mixture.

I soon found out that these three sisters owned the school. They were noble ladies, and like so many ladies of the German nobility, they had been forced to work for a livelihood, owing to the possible extravagance of father or brothers. The eldest sister, Fräulein Elizabeth, was a qualified teacher. Fraulein Marie was an artist, and gave lessons in painting and singing. Fraulein Toni was the Hausfrau, and supervised the domestic side of the establishment. She was really beautiful, and must have been a 'Juno' in her young days. She was tall and stately. The only members that seemed out of harmony with the rest of her person were her hands. They were large and red, for they had done real hard work. She was such a mother to the youngest children that they called her Auntie Toni. She always sat at one end of the long table already mentioned, and did the carving. Somewhat flustered and flushed by the part she had played in the preparation of the excellent meal, she eyed her big joint with relish and satisfaction, and cut generous slices for the hungry people around her. There was no stinting and everything was the best.

At the other end of the table sat Fraulein Elizabeth, the Principal, with Fraulein Marie at her right. I used to admire the energetic way in which these two kept the conversation going, between copious mouthfuls. Only English or French was spoken, according to the day, and I found it a strain to pipe out my English contribution to the conversation on English days, so what must it have meant to them? Their English was quite good, though amusing at times. They always made three syllables of words like 'carriage' and 'marriage'. The old custom (traditional in the great houses) of the *Gesegnete Mahlzeit* was kept up here. After dinner, we all filed around in solemn procession to the 'Head of the table', in this case, Fraulein Elizabeth, kissed her proffered hand, and said '*Gesegnete Mahlzeit*' (Blest meal-time). The children curtsied, and I bowed my stiff little English bow. I thought it a quaint and pretty custom. The children did it to their parents at home, and so it was a touch of home life.

At the side of the house was a pretty little garden and lawn, where you could sit and read in peace. At the back of it stood the school, and beyond it the playground. There was a large walnut tree just beyond the playground. How I enjoyed those windfall walnuts when the autumn came! They tasted of home and reminded me of my mother who loved them. She always bought them when they were in season. The school struck me as being big, cold and bare, so different from our pretty school at home. It was well equipped and there was a full and efficient staff of mistresses. Renowned professors came to the senior classes for History and Literature, and the Lutheran Pastor for Religion.

I threw myself into my new work with all the ardour I could command, but it was irksome to me and I disliked it. Secretly I was rather afraid of the children. Many of them were nearly as old as I was, just finishing off their education prior to making their debut into the great world, and there lurked always a secret fear lest I should not be able to manage them. What astonished me was my homesickness which hung over me like a heavy pall. I had never dreamed I should be homesick but I was, terribly. How ever could I endure a whole year in such depression and misery? 'You are here now', I told myself, 'and you must go through with it.' After the first month it was not so bad, and eleven months seemed so very much less than a year.

The day pupils were easier to manage than the boarders, and several of them soon made friends with me and would invite me to go to their beautiful and stately homes and have tea with them. That was quite pleasant, and so were the long walks I used to take into the country, alone, as a rule, ignoring the fact that girls of my age were not supposed to take walks alone. What I missed more than anything was my Anglican Church. On Sundays I went to the Lutheran Church, but it was deadly cold and gloomy. Occasionally, on a wet day, I used to drop into the Catholic Church, of which the doors always were open, and there I would kneel down and pray quietly, feeling somehow more at home than in the chill gloom of the Lutheran Church, but I never went to Mass or any service in the Catholic Church.

One event stands out prominently in that first year, it was the Imperial Manoeuvres, which were held in the surrounding countryside. The streets were gaily decorated, and were absolutely alive with haughty looking officers and soldiers of all ranks. I never saw anything in my life to equal it. The Kaiser and Kaiserin were the guests of two of my pupils, whose father was the Governor of the Province, so to him fell the honour of entertaining the Imperial couple. We used to wave to them from the windows as they passed to and fro, and call out 'Hoch!' We also saw the Kaiser's chief guests, the ill-fated Czar and Czarina, Nicholas II and his wife, Alice of Hesse, a grand daughter of Queen Victoria. Little did I think how tragic would be their end in the far-off Siberian prison!

At the end of the Summer Term, I heard with consternation and regret that Fräulein Von Vogden was selling her house and school, and was going to retire. She and her sisters were now middle-aged, they had worked hard and constantly hoped to spend the rest of their lives in leisure and peace. They loved Switzerland, and had settled on that beauty spot for their new home, having purchased a villa on the shore of Lake Geneva. Well did they deserve their lot, for they were good, kind and benevolent. I was fond of them and they of me, and we were sorry to have to part. Their memory has a warm place in my heart.

I spent the summer holidays at Hermsdorf near Waldenburg, with relatives of my brother's great friend. We were quite near the Riesengebirge, and made most interesting excursions into them and the beautiful countryside. Once we went into Bohemia. I was touched at seeing the children curtsy as they passes us, saying in German, 'Praised be Jesus Christ'. 'What a beautiful Catholic custom', I thought.

My German made big strides at Hermsdorf, as I heard and spoke nothing but that language, still I was not content with the slow progress I had made, and after having spent the Christmas term with Fraulein Von Vogden's successors, I resolved to make a change. I gladly accepted a post as English companion to one of Fraulein Von Vogden's earlier pupils, Katherina Von Walther, who lived with her mother and father in a remote place some ten or twelve miles from Oels. I was to be treated as a daughter, read and speak English with

Katherina in the morning, and be free for the rest of the day, and receive the same dress allowance as Katherina.

I was really delighted at the prospect. To be far away in the country, and to see home life in Germany, held real attractions for me. So I went there in the early days of January. Shall I ever forget the long, snowy journey? The family brougham was at the station to meet me. The tall liveried coachman almost scared me; he looked so much like a Tartar. Over his silver-buttoned coat, he wore a heavy black fur cape fastened tightly below the chin, and a big fur cap to match, which was drawn so low over the face and ears, that, between the cape and the cap, there was not much of him to be seen. In such wintry weather no one, of course, could be expected to come to meet me, so I was alone in the big, cold brougham, and my grim driver on the box. Hour after hour we drove on in the snow. No town, no village seemed to appear, but occasionally we passed what looked like the lights of a gate lodge, and then on again into the silence and darkness. Each time we passed these rare gate lodges, I said to myself, 'Here we are'. It became uncanny. Had I been kidnapped, and was I being driven off to Siberia?

At last, after what seemed to be five or six hours, but which was perhaps two, we did stop, and it was before a long low, quaint old house, called a castle, but not like one in appearance. I received a warm welcome from Herr and Frau Von Walther and Katherina, and at once I felt at home and contented. My room was large and sunny, with windows on two sides. A cozy sofa in the centre of the room looked homelike and inviting, and there was a very nice writing desk near one of the windows. Everything in that house went like clockwork, and I soon saw that my hostess was a perfect *Hausfrau*. Breakfast was served in the big, austere-looking dining room. We four looked lost in it.

We never went there except for meals. A nice little boy-in-buttons waited on us. At breakfast he brought in delicious hot rolls. These were broken open, the interior removed, and the warm crisp crust was eaten with butter. In Görlitz, we had to eat them dry! Though in reality they were not dry, for everyone dipped them in the coffee!

At the end of breakfast, my hostess always produced a book from the small basket of keys which never left her, and began to read a beautiful meditation aloud, and at the end of which, she said the Our Father reverently and devoutly. She was a good woman and a conscientious wife and mother. With her basket of keys in hand, she would go off to the kitchen quarters, order dinner, give out supplies, and look after things in general. Then, a little later, she would often join us in her sitting room, or in Katherina's sanctum, built by her father to welcome her home for good when Fraulein Von Vogden's boarding school had finished with her. What a kind thought it was, and how prettily and even lavishly they had furnished it. Here she entertained her girl friends on the rather rare occasions they visited her, there too she wrote, read and did her embroidery.

In the middle of the long morning, the boy-in-buttons, Herman, would appear with a silver salver on which were arranged sandwiches of various kinds, and glasses of delicious milk. This was 'second breakfast', which certainly was a more substantial meal than the first breakfast had been, and which sustained us until the rather late dinner, somewhere about one o' clock, possibly later. This was the principal meal of the day, as we did not dine in the evening, except when there was a large, formal dinner party given. When Herr Von Walther was present, a lively conversation was kept up in German; when he was not there, we spoke English. He and I were very good friends. He enjoyed teasing me about English politics, but all the time I knew he secretly admired England. I smiled at his funny pronunciation of the various politicians. Among others, I remember that Mr. Joseph Chamberlain was always pronounced to rhyme with 'hammer-lan'. After dinner, we went for a stroll or I went to my room to read German, or write the very long and detailed letters home.

As regularly as clockwork every evening after supper, we used to pay a visit to Herr Von Walther's dear old father, and his two unmarried sisters, who lived a stone's throw from us in what was called 'the new castle': we lived in the old one. The old gentleman, quite patriarchal in appearance, was exceedingly interesting. He enjoyed talking to me about England, and about great English books he had read. This nightly visit was spoiled for me by the excess of rank tobacco smoke with which the room was filled. My clothes reeked of it, and it was so blinding, and so suffocating, that I used to long for the time of departure

So the days passed, one being astonishingly like the other; yet they were never monotonous. There were young girls of Katherina's age at three of the neighbouring castles, and those we used to meet at tennis, or tea parties at their houses or ours. We met them too at the stately dinners and dances given during the season. These were novel and exciting. One stands out in my memory, because the snow being so thick, we had to go in a sleigh, and it was my first sleigh drive. Just now I used the expression 'neighbouring castles'. They were miles apart, so this sleigh drive through wild, snowy country was a long one. I was impressed by the solemn silence all round, save for our sleigh bells. As the sun sank, the snow was no longer white, but a most lovely pink. It was a scene of great beauty and I shall never forget it. Nor shall I forget the piercing cold of that drive. The coachman had tucked us up most carefully, but in spite of that I was perished.

About once a month, Katherina and I used to drive to the quaint little town of Oels for her painting lesson. The town was a long way off and so it was evening before we were home again. It was quite strange being in a town again, and though I enjoyed the change, I was always glad to get back to the country. The spring-time was lovely, after the long, silent winter. I used to be up with the lark and practice before breakfast. I remember learning Mendelssohn's *Spring Song* by heart. My year in Germany was coming to an end, and surely I might count on the longed-for return home. Yet every one dissuaded me from leaving so soon. 'Your German has improved so wonderfully', said Herr Von Walther, 'what a pity not to stay a little longer until you are really proficient in it.' I knew he was right. I could not afford to go home for a holiday and return to Germany. After a sharp struggle, I decided to stay on; it was no good half doing a thing. I had only one ambition, and that was to perfect my German and French, then to return to my old school and work side by side with Mary, near my dear ones, to the end of my days!

I shall never forget the kindness of the Von Walthers towards me. They did all they could to give me pleasure; indeed they spoiled me. A few years later, when Katharina was happily married, Frau Von Walther wrote to ask me to go to them for good, as their adopted daughter.

In the autumn of that same year, Katherina was to pay a prolonged visit to some of her friends. I had been with her several months and her English was now very good, so I was free to accept the invitation given me by some of her friends in one of the neighbouring castles to go to them for a few months. This I did, and my stay with them was to be another weighty milestone along life's strange path. I knew the girls, of course, as I had often met them at Katherina's home, and at dinner parties. There were only two girls at home, Cara and Tosca; their sister and two brothers were still at school.

Chapter 3

The Von Gilgenheimb family lived in a large house, called of course, a castle, in the middle of their large estate. The grounds were beautiful, and the walks in them a delight. Not far from the castle there was a quiet enclosure surrounded by yew trees. Here their father was buried, and here they were always going to pray at his grave. They were Catholics and staunch ones. Their father, a cavalry officer, had died suddenly, before his prime, and the family seemed unable to recover from the blow. Frau Von Gilgenheimb was deeply affected by the death of her husband, and her mother, Countess Matuschka, had come to live with her and cheer her in her lonely widowhood. They were both kind and attentive, but there was always a certain aloofness which chilled after the perfectly homely life I had led with Katherina. The girls were handsome, as their mother still was, in fact Tosca was a beauty. I used to think how an artist would love to paint her, and catch, if possible, the pure and spiritual loveliness of her face. Both girls had been educated at the Ursuline Convent in Braslau, where their father's sister was a nun. Their younger sister, Dagmar, was still there. They loved the convent and its associations, and would never tire of talking about it.

In front of the castle there was a large lake with swans on it. It was my delight to play with these swans, and I used to call out 'Hans, Hans!', and the male swan would sail majestically towards me and condescend to accept the food I threw to him. There was a boat on the lake, and for hours at a time, I would sit in it, listen to the play of the waters from the enclosed trout streams, and read German aloud. 'What a clever idea', I thought, 'to keep these poor trout enclosed in such a way that they can be netted and caught, whenever needed'. I had heard Frau Von Gilgenheimb exclaim once: - 'How inconsiderate of Colonel "X" to choose Friday for his visit. He knows we are Catholics, and must also know the difficulty of providing an abstinence dinner in this remote spot. If we were in town it would not matter. Ask the gardener to catch some trout, and then with a good soup and omelettes, we shall have to manage'. So the poor trout appeared as a lordly dish, and the lunch was a success.

It is very strange, but I have no recollection whatsoever of ever driving to church on Sundays, while I was with the Von Walthers, and yet they were such good people. Probably the distance was so great that Herr Von Walther refused to tire his horses with the long jaunt. With the Gilgenheimbs it was different. Every Sunday we drove off to church in a curious vehicle. To me it looked like an old-fashioned omnibus cut in half! It was more than twice the size of a brougham. The seats were placed as they are in a bus, and easily held ten persons. The coachman would put me down at the Lutheran Church, and then drive on a little further with the family to the Catholic Church. Our service must have been finished first, because I distinctly remember standing in the porch of the Catholic Church from which I could see the children in front of the altar singing with heart and soul the German translation of the *Agnus Dei*. I noticed too that at the words 'Have mercy on us', they reverently smote their breasts. 'That seems to be real worship', was my comment. How different from that lifeless Lutheran service I had just come from. But not for worlds would I have admitted this to the Gilgenheimbs. Occasionally the girls and I had long discussions about religion, and somehow I used to get the best of the arguments. This was probable because I could express myself more easily than they could. They were amazed at the 'Branch Theory' (i.e. that the Catholic Church, the Greek Church and the Anglican Church were the three branches of the universal Church), and no wonder! If they had been smarter, they would have asked: - 'And where does the Lutheran Church come in? Is it a twig?'

By this time I could speak German almost as fluently as my own tongue, and to my delight, I found that at last I was dreaming in German. That had been my ambition and I had promised myself that when I could do that, I might conscientiously begin to think of home. It would not take long to rub up my French, as I heard so much of it now. French was always spoken at table when the waiter was present. Three months constant study and practice in France would surely be enough. Then home and friends, and no more separation.

Somehow, unconsciously, I had built up another Fool's Paradise. Like the earlier one, it was doomed to destruction. Never shall I forget that afternoon. Tosca and I were alone, and we were playing duets from Wagner's operas, as we so often did. The maid brought us both letters. I must have made some exclamation of pain, for Tosca looked up from her letter, saying:- 'Why, what's the matter? Have you bad news'. I think I did try to explain to her, but failed. How could she fathom the full meaning of the devastating news I had just received. It was so simple and commonplace - merely a letter from the Head Mistress of my old school, telling me not to entertain the idea of rejoining the staff there, as there was no vacancy. There was, I think, a sort of hint that I was qualified for something better. That was all, but to me it was a terrible upheaval, and in fact, it changed the whole course of my life.

I was in an abyss of misery, too stunned to think. But gradually, thoughts began to shape themselves, at first incoherently, then definitely; - 'My old life is at an end, that is certain,' I told myself. 'There is nothing stable on this earth. The old hymn is still true than, "Change is our portion here". God alone does not change. He is the only reality, the only strength and stay in life. Outside Him is no real happiness. What happiness there is, is three parts pain, because it is fleeting. If two love each other, separation or death will come. Life is a mystery and a sad one'. So my thoughts ran on. Sunshine had gone out of my life; it was dark, but in the darkness I clung to God.

Not long after this, Frau Von Gilgenheimb proposed a few days holiday in Braslau. There was shopping to be done, the nuns to be visited, and a famous circus to be seen. The girls were delighted at the prospect and I too was grateful for the change. Only three things remain in my mind of those few days; - the circus, which was thrilling, Mass at the Church, and the visit to the convent. Rather a strange mixture!

'I shan't know what to do, when I stand, and when to kneel.' I had said to Tosca as we entered the church. 'I'll nudge you', she said. She also shared her missal with me, but the priest was going much more quickly than I could follow, and Tosca turned the page before I had half finished, so it was not a successful arrangement. 'This is a hotchpotch,' I thought, 'I can't make head or tail of it'.

Now for the visit to the convent. I was all eagerness to see and speak to a nun. Never in my life had I been near a convent or a nun, so this would be a thrilling experience. And indeed it was. I remember every detail of that memorable visit, nearly fifty years ago. The convent stood in the heart of the town, and the imposing convent church looked quaint and old. A white-veiled Sister opened the door, and on recognising our party, she smiled and said, 'Praised be Jesus Christ', to which the girls answered, 'For ever and ever. Amen.'

We went down to a cloister. White veiled and black veiled nuns were flitting busily, but quietly about. Then something strange happened, strange because I had never experienced anything like it before, and only once since. It was a masterful and overwhelming conviction that seized hold of me - 'this is the life for me'. It was definite, simple and irresistible.

Cara and Tosca introduced me to their favourite nuns; I thought them charming. Tosca told Mater Margaretha of my wish to go to Paris to polish up my French. On hearing that I had no friends there to guide or advise me, she strongly disapproved. 'Why not go to one of the Ursuline Convents in Belgium?' she said after a pause. 'I know one of them very well indeed, for I was exiled there during Bismarck's Kultur-Kampf.' I jumped eagerly at the idea, especially when I found that my slender purse could easily manage the low fees charged by that convent. Then and there I resolved to write for a prospectus as soon as we returned home.

The girls loved every stone of the place, and begged to have dinner in the school refectory, as of old. So a simple dinner was served to us there, while the elders of our party were sumptuously served in the parlour. I remember we had turnips as a vegetable, and they were most delicious. Strange that such an item should have remained in my memory! In the evening we went to Benediction in the great church. Tosca explained that the nuns were in the gallery, but we could not see them because of their enclosure. I knew they were there worshipping with all their soul, and this thought enhanced the awe and beauty of that service. I was sorry when it was over; I could have stayed on forever! So ended our brief Braslau holiday.

We returned to the castle and took up the daily routine of reading, playing duets, singing and walking. There was an extraordinary sameness about those days. Then the gong sounded for meals, we assembled in the drawing room, and there the procession would line up, two and two. Quite solemnly we filed throughout the deserted billiard room and a suite of small rooms leading out of each other without a door (as far as I can remember) into the austere-looking dining room and this was repeated day after day.

But my stay with the Von Gilgenheimbs was drawing to a close. I had to say goodbye to so many kind friends who had made my long stay in their country so very pleasant. How fortunate I had been in meeting with such good and kind people! They count among the nicest it has been my lot to meet.

Meanwhile, I had been corresponding with the Ursuline nuns of Lierre, near Antwerp, and it was settled that I should become a pupil there in January, 1898. The remaining weeks I spent in Görlitz. At the pressing invitation of Frau Von Walther's cousin, I spent the last of my German days with him in Berlin. He was extremely kind, showed me the sights of that great city, took me down the famous street 'Unter den Linden'. And finally, after having loaded me with good things, saw me off in the night train bound for Holland and Belgium.

Since my visit to Braslau, some of my old buoyance had returned. The future was shaping itself, and perhaps after all, it would not be so lonely as I imagined. At least, I was nearing home, a few months more and I should be there. I was quite excited and amused too at the thought of putting down my hair and being a schoolgirl once again. I liked the idea for I disliked getting old. So life was beginning to look rosy again.

Chapter 4

The nuns at Lierre gave me a warm welcome and I felt at home at once, and soon grew to love the place. I worked hard at my French, and soon spoke it fluently. It was so much easier than German. As I walked round the playground, I could see the nuns in the adjacent garden, walking up and down in noisy sabots, reading or saying their rosary. I liked to watch them. 'Those nuns have solved the riddle of life', I used to think, 'they are happy because they have given themselves and all they hold dear to God. I wish I were one of them'. But I was too practical to let my mind dwell on what seemed a shear impossibility.

When I saw the Grotto of Lourdes at the end of the garden, I recalled with interest all that I heard and read about it. I must have read a brochure of Zola on the subject, but what had most interested and captivated me was a description written about it by Mr. Grist, M.A., the Head Master of one of the boys' schools at home. Summer after summer he used to go for long walking tours through different parts of Europe, and he would send vivid and remarkably interesting accounts of these walks to our local newspaper. One of these articles was about Lourdes, and it had delighted me. He, evidently, was no believer in the miraculous, neither was I, he just stated what he saw. One important fact, however, he did observe and I remembered it, and verified it more than forty years later when I went to Lourdes myself. 'Two worlds meet in Lourdes,' was his remark, so he must have sensed the supernatural world to some extent. One sparkling little incident recounted by him amused me at the time, and amuses me still. He related it in a charming manner that I fear I cannot reproduce. On one of the countless booths which line the narrow streets of Lourdes, he noticed among a hundred other things, a number of neat little leather cases, holding one up to the dark-eyed shop girl, he asked, 'For cigarettes, Mademoiselle?' 'Not at all, sir, they are to hold rosaries', came the answer from the amused and astonished shop-girl.

Quite often the children would speak of Lourdes. Some of their sisters went there on a pilgrimage. One very nice child was telling me about her tiny sister whom she idolized. 'She was dying', she said, 'Mother took her to Lourdes, and the Blessed Mother cured her'. It was the perfect simplicity, perfect faith and the almost matter-of-fact way in which she told me that impressed me. To her, at least, and to her family, the miraculous was an understood thing, thought I, and I began to wonder.

The convent chapel was not beautiful, but I loved to be in it. I thought the evening prayers were impressive, and I soon learned them by heart. But on the whole, I cannot remember being attracted in any strong way by Catholic worship as I saw it there. I was attracted by the patient, self-denying life of the nuns; also I became much attached to two of them.

Then came the month of May, and things changed. When in Germany I had heard Tosca speak of the lovely month of May, and of the '*Maindacht*', a beautiful expression in German. It is badly rendered in English by 'May devotions'. Therefore, I was not surprised to hear there would be May devotions every evening, followed by Benediction. I was delighted at this, for I loved evening Benediction. So every evening, the Community and children would assemble in chapel, and one of the nuns would read a sort of simple homily about our Lady, followed by a short episode, such as her apparition to Bernadette at Lourdes, and always ending with the words: - '*Car elle est Notre Mere, Ecce Mater Tua*'. (For she is our Mother. Behold thy Mother).

Night after night these words impressed me; night and day they haunted me, I wish I could describe to what extent.

No doubt it was the ever-present heartache at my dear mother's death which helped to etch these words on my very soul. 'These Catholics all around me have Mary for their Mother, why is she denied to me? Christ is the Saviour of all, then surely his Mother was too'. I felt I had been robbed of a consoling birthright. I was much disturbed in mind, and began to question the nuns. I read Henri Lasserre's beautiful book on Lourdes. I saw then that it was a historical fact - this story of Lourdes. The Emperor Napoleon and the Empress Eugenie had been connected with it. State documents proved the truth of it. When asked her name, the Blessed Mother said:- 'I am the Immaculate Conception'. That was passing strange. It clinched the argument.

If the story of the Apparition were true (and I now believed it was), then the dogma of the Immaculate Conception was true also. All the teaching of the Catholic Church might be true, and she might be the depository of the teaching of Christ. I remembered going down the garden alone to the Grotto, and saying something very child-like to the Blessed Mother. Something like:- 'Please be my mother, and show me what is right, and help me to do it'. She did help, for gradually doubts and difficulties vanished, and I saw that the Catholic Church was Christ's true Church, and I must join it.

Gradually three ideas took shape in my mind. The first was that this step would mean a definite cleavage with the past; the second was that I must not act precipitately for fear the dear ones at home should have the additional pain of thinking this step was the result of infatuation; the third was that I could never bear to go home again. The sacrifice entailed was a supreme one, and I cannot write of it. I also knew that if I made this sacrifice, I should be a nun. That remarkable conviction that came to me so suddenly at the Ursuline Convent in Braslau would be realised.

By Strange Paths

I must have spoken to the Reverend Mother about my plan to remain in Belgium, for she offered to allow me to stay on, free of charge as long as I liked. This I gladly accepted, as my purse was growing empty. The difficulty now was how to tell the dear ones at home, and my friend Mary? They would be unspeakably shocked, and Mary would think I had failed to keep tryst. I told my dear sister when she came to see me at Lierre. She said she was not much surprised; she was not hurt for she knew I should not do anything I did not consider the right thing to do. This consoled me tremendously for she was so dear to me that the thought of paining her was unbearable. My father and my brother were much upset and wrote me letters that hurt. My mind was made up. I should ask to be instructed and then received into the Catholic Church, and then seek a position as English Governess for the time being.

The summer holidays ended in September. Towards the middle of the month I received a wire from my brother, saying he had to go to Hamburg and would call to see me on his way back. This unexpected visit filled me with consternation. Was this then to be the meeting I had looked forward to so eagerly and for so long? He arrived and I remember walking round the garden with him. He was very stern, and the conversation was strained. 'Ask Reverend Mother to allow you to take me round the town,' he said, suddenly. The permission was given at once.

'You had better take off that white muslin frock', said Reverend Mother, 'it would attract too much attention here.' I had put on this frock, thinking it would please my brother. So we went round the quaint town, examining some antiques which interested my brother. As we passed a hotel, he said, rather abruptly, 'I want to go in here. Do you mind waiting downstairs while I go up?' So I waited, wondering what his business could be. When he came down it was time for his train, so we walked to the station together. He then begged me to go home with him, hinting that he might be able to send me to the university to graduate there.

'No', I said quietly, 'I am not going home. I shall earn my living here'. He paced up and down the platform. There were tears in his eyes. I had never seen them there before. He jerked out something to this effect:- 'To think that a sister of mine should have got into the claws of the Catholic Church. There's no power on earth, not even the Pope of Rome, who shall prevent me from getting her out of those claws. I don't care if I go to prison for it.' The train steamed in. I was so stunned by this unexpected burst of passion from my undemonstrative brother that I did not understand the force of his words. So when he said:- 'I can't kiss you goodbye before this crowd, jump in the train and kiss me there,' I obliged meekly. He followed me, slammed the door, and said, 'Choose quickly, either you promise me to come home in three months, or I shall take you with me now'. I answered quite calmly:- 'I have told you I will not go home. I shall become a Catholic and work here'. He sat down beside me, the train whistled and we were off.

His face was working and his voice trembled as he said, 'I've done many a bad thing in my life, but I believe I'm doing a good thing now. I promised father not to come home without you. I arranged matters with my bank in the hotel this afternoon, so if I am pursued and imprisoned, all will be in order'. I said, 'I know you are doing this for love of me, but you don't know what you are doing, or what this means to me'. I did not cry, but I trembled from head to foot from the shock. He felt it and put his arm around me to steady me. He tried to console me, and did console me by telling me that I was to stay with my friend, Mary, until things shaped themselves. But what kind of welcome would she give me? Poor Mary! I had betrayed her trust. Presently, I said to my brother:- 'there is one thing I must insist upon, and it is this - before we embark, you must wire to the nuns that you have forced me away. I insist on the word "forced". Just think what a state of mind they will be in tonight. As a great exception Reverend Mother let me go out with you, and this is the result'. He promised to do as I wished, and the wire was sent, but not before the poor nuns had lived through hours of anxiety.

The September evening was chilly, and I was lightly clad. My brother bought me a nice, warm travelling rug in Antwerp, and wrapped me up in it as we sat on deck and watched the moon rising. He was all kindness to me now, and I responded to it. I was always a bad sailor, and in the morning I must have presented a sorry spectacle. 'Can't you do something with your hair?' he said, 'it has come down'. I had not even a pocket comb with me, and I felt too ill to raise my arms, but I tried to do something with my dishevelled locks. I was wearing a light green skirt and bolero, and a white silk, sleeveless sort of blouse. This was now soiled, but as I only had the clothes I wore, I could not alter this. In this condition, I arrived at Mary's house, feeling very much like a runaway dog being whipped home, his tail between his legs. Both Mary and her mother were very kind to me, but they were bitterly disappointed, and things were strained.

I shall never forget meeting my dear old father. He only said one word, but I knew what it meant. He just said, 'Ah', and folded me in his arms. Such cherished dreams I had had of my homecoming! Where were they now? Almost immediately my brother took me to one of the big shops, to rig me out from top to toe. My spirits rose when I felt less bedraggled. Feminine vanity! But a promise made by my brother cheered me more than anything else. This is what he said, 'I know how impressionable you are, and I really believe those nuns have captivated you. If, however, I find I am mistaken, and if after three months you have not changed your mind, I will pay your expenses to Lierre, and you may do what you like, provided it be of your own free will'.

This was magnanimous, and hope returned. My brother was devoted to me, and did all he could to entertain me, and to distract me from my obsession. At least the three months passed, and I returned to Lierre for the Christmas Holidays. The bliss of that return. On the feast of St. Thomas of Canterbury, I was privately confirmed by his Eminence, Cardinal Goossens, in his chapel at his place in Malines. It seemed to me I never had been so happy before. I walked on air, and every step echoed, 'I am a Catholic'. The nuns would have liked me to enter there and then, but I knew it was better to wait another year so that my dear ones might get used to the idea; also I wanted to earn some money to pay for my trousseau. My certificates replaced a dowry, but I could not bear the thought of entering without a penny, though Reverend Mother assured me that did not matter. 'A proud heart and a beggars purse', had been Mother's description of me.

Without much difficulty I obtained a post at the Convent of Our Lady of Sion, Bayswater. It was an imposing building, near Kensington Gardens, and besides the Convent proper, contained two schools, a High School for day pupils and a boarding school. Among several very interesting children there were two daughters of Wilfred and Alice Meynell, Viola and Olivia. The mistresses taught in both schools. Everyone was kind, but I did not relish my work somehow, and was always glad when school hours were over. The nuns often talked to me, and I think they would have liked me to enter there, but my heart was set elsewhere. I was so happy to be a Catholic, and to be under the same roof as our Divine Lord. I loved to go to the chapel, and at odd times, if anyone wanted me, it was there I was to be found.

The long summer holidays I spent at Lierre, a couple of the shorter ones with my dear Auntie Lucan or my cousin Clara, both very dear to me. My Auntie was one of the noblest and bravest women I have known. They were most kind about my change in religion, and made no reproach.

The September term of that year, 1899, was a memorable one for many reasons; it was my farewell to the world and it brought me the life-long friendship of one of the mistresses, Miss O'Callaghan. For more than six months we had lived and taught side by side, but always at elbow's distance. In fact, I thought she positively disliked me because I had usurped, as it were, the place of her dearest friend, who, soon after leaving Bayswater, became a Benedictine at Princethorpe, near Rugby. Quite suddenly, a deep and lasting friendship sprang up between us, all the deeper because each of us knew that in a few short weeks, separation must come. We spent all our leisure time together. She had a heart of gold, and I loved her with a deep and lasting affection.

My sister's conversion was the answer to earnest prayer. I felt I could not leave her alone in the world unless she were a Catholic, for then she would have the all-powerful and sustaining consolation of the sacraments. So I asked the Blessed Mother to guide her into the Church, as she had guided me, and then, with a clear conscience, I could leave her behind and enter the convent. It was just the half-term holiday, so I was able to go to Bradford, where she was living, and be present at her Baptism and First Holy Communion. My gratitude for this answer to prayer was unbounded. On the night of her First Communion day I had to tell her that I was going to be a nun. She knew at once what it cost me to tell her, and begged me not to be upset, that she had half expected it, and was so glad for my sake. She was so sweet about it, and so understanding, that the grief of the morrow's parting lost much of its sting.

On my way home from Bradford to London, I broke my journey at Lincoln, that I might spend an hour or two with my dear old Head Mistress, formerly Miss Bebbington, who lived there with her husband and two children. I knew it would be my last visit to her, but she did not. The visit left a sad impression, and again I thought her married life was not what she expected. She wore her arm in a sling, for that terrible malady, neuritis, had begun to undermine her strength. Later on, she became a confirmed invalid, poor dear. My heart was wrung with pity for her when, some twelve years later, a terrible calamity wrecked her life. Then I broke the long silence of years and wrote to her.

What happened was this:- Her only daughter, Dorothy, whom she idolized, was just about to go up to Newnham College, Cambridge, to begin her Tripos course, as her mother had done before her, when the doctor suggested that it might be wise to have her appendix removed before going, in case the slight pain in her side should develop and interrupt her studies. The advice was taken, and Dorothy went to the Hospital. Her mother stayed quite near, and actually saw her going along the corridor to the operating theatre. Ether was given to her, but before the surgeon touched her with his knife, a twitch near the heart was noticed, the pulse stopped, and Dorothy was dead. The poor heartbroken mother answered my letter, and from that time until her death many years later, I always wrote to her once or twice a year. It cheered her to know her 'Old Girls' sympathized with her. Her last letter, written in pencil, was only just legible, for she had become so crippled that all she could do was to hold the pencil between her second and third fingers and try to guide it as best she could. She assured me of her 'undying love'. She will always have my undying gratitude. R.I.P.

Not long after that memorable visit to the North, my brother volunteered for the Boer War, and left for South Africa. I knew he was thoroughly disappointed in me and the world in general. In a gloomy mood he embarked for South Africa.

None of my good friends knew I was going to be a nun, though all of then seemed to guess what my vocation would be, so I had no painful goodbyes to face, except my goodbye to Miss O'Callaghan. That was a wrench I shall never forget, it was a terrible one.

I began to feel that I should never reach Lierre. When, eventually, I did get there a day or two before Christmas, I was quite worn out by the suffering of those last weeks. It was on Christmas Eve, the first anniversary of my Baptism, that I entered the Novitiate. I knew the Novice Mistress very well, and loved and respected her, so I soon felt at home. At times I could hardly realize I had reached my goal at last. There was no elation, no exuberance, but only the simple reality that I was in God's house, and that I had given myself to Him. One day, soon after my arrival, my Novice Mistress surprised me by asking me to help her take the inventory of my trousseau. Seeing my surprise, she explained that this was always done, in case a postulant should not persevere. The thought that I might be a failure had never once crossed my mind, so sure of myself was I.

Just three months after I had entered, my dear friend, Miss O'Callaghan paid me her promised visit. How I had looked forward to it, and how I loved being with her again! She stayed a few days, and then came the inevitable goodbye, which we thought was going to be a final one. Soon after her visit, she went to Princethorpe, where she eventually entered.

Chapter 5

Now it happened that most of the Ursuline Convents of Flanders, with their affiliations in England used to send their postulants for one year's training to the General Novitiate at Raecht. That meant that their clothing took place there. Hearing all the novices speak rapturously of their novitiate there, I was naturally very eager for the time to come when I too might go there. I went in April with my twin postulant, and at once felt in my element. I do not think I was in my element in Lierre. The life at Raecht was given up to spirituality, and that was what I loved: of course, there was housework to be done, but not very much. A most interesting conference was given daily on the Holy Rule and constitutions by the very competent Novice Mistress. The Chaplain gave lessons on Christian doctrine. Lessons were given by some of the older novices to the younger ones on such subjects as Church work, embroidery and languages.

No novice taught in the National School attached to the Convent. As the windows were high up, we never caught a glimpse of the outside world, we were completely enclosed, and I loved it. I think no Carmelite Novitiate could have enjoyed a greater solitude. The sweet month of May brought with it the retreat preparatory to the clothing, which took place privately on 5 June 1900. How intense was my joy at being a nun at last. It was a delight to wake in the morning and see the holy habit waiting to be put on, so that another day might be spent in God's service. Those were, indeed, happy days, the happiest I had known since my girlhood.

My happiness soon received a sudden shock, for news came through the War Office that my dear brother had been killed in action. For one whole day and night I was overcome by sorrow. Then, to my intense relief, news came that an error had been made. My brother was a prisoner of war, but had not been killed. How immense was my gratitude!

The months passed, and I became more and more deeply attached to this almost cloistered life, so much so that I began to dread the thought of leaving it. I do not think I told anyone, not even my Novice Mistress, in whom I had confided any difficulties that arose. Her explanations had always been most helpful, but this new dread I could not speak of; I was ashamed of it, it seemed so ungrateful and unreasonable. It was just a sacrifice that had to be made, and the less said about it the better. So when my superiors came to bring us home to Lierre, they saw nothing of my interior struggle. I think I told them later.

The religious life now began for me in earnest. I was at once put on the school staff, and spent many hours in teaching and in supervising. I felt no joy in my work, except the dry sort of joy of having tried to do my duty. I knew, of course, that the one thing necessary was to do the best I could with the work assigned to me. I knew, too, there was more merit in doing work that was repugnant. I understood the theory, but lacked the generosity and virtue needed to put it into practice. Deep down in my heart there was always a quiet happiness, or rather, peace of soul because I had given myself to God. I was His, and always would be. Nothing ever shook that conviction; it was the surface of the soul that was perplexed and, perhaps, disappointed, though at the time I do not think I admitted this myself.

It may have been the result of this perplexity that I had a strange experience on the eve of my Holy Profession. A most painful sense of utter unworthiness to be professed overpowered me quite suddenly. It was no false humility, it may have been the work of the devil. What ever it was, it was a terrible experience. My Novice Mistress saw at once something was wrong, and asked me if I were ill. I burst into tears and sobbed out that the two other novices were worthy, but Holy Profession was not for me. Amazed to see me in this state, (I was invariably calm and self-possessed, even matter-of-fact), she took me in her arms and tried to comfort me. She reassured me somewhat by telling me that my vocation was a solid one, she had studied me for three years, the Community had given me their votes, then why should I repine? This fear of making my vows was a temptation, and I must not listen to it. Later on, that same evening, she told me she had spoken to our Chaplain on the subject. 'Tell her from me', he said, 'that if one of the three is worthy, it is she'. So the next morning I was professed with the two others. I was now solemnly consecrated to God, and nothing else mattered.

Every summer brought the joy of a lengthy visit from my dear sister. Reverend Mother most kindly allowed her to spend her holidays with us. We were able to spend long hours at the end of the garden. I did needlework and she chatted or read. How she loved the cherry walk! The whole wall was covered with delicious Morello cherries and as we sat on the seat under them, the luscious, deep red fruit dangled over our heads. She could not resist them, and many a one found its way into her eager mouth!

My dear brother came to see me too. He was so changed in his attitude towards me. He was quite interested in all I could tell him of our life, and he was extremely kind and sympathetic, and we seemed to be living the old times once again. Not long after this, he wrote me a beautiful letter in which he said he no longer regarded the step I had taken as a dire calamity. He was proud of me, I should always be enshrined in his memory. This gave me great joy.

The outstanding event of the year to which I always looked forward eagerly and hungrily was our annual retreat. I loved it. Then, and then alone, I was in my element. The meditations were beautiful, and always provided food for much thought, but unfortunately, there was not much solitude or time left for private prayer. It was always with a pang that I said goodbye to retreat, to take up again, bravely and resolutely the cross of every day life.

Before every great feast, it was the custom for the Community to assemble and listen to the reading of a book suitable to the occasion. Strangely enough, the book chosen was most often *The Liturgical Year*. I say 'strangely enough', for it was strange, as the liturgical life and liturgical books were almost unknown there until this book was introduced. To ask for a book containing the ceremonies of Holy Week, as I did when a postulant, was an innovation, and was, at first, refused. No one had a missal until I received one from my dear brother. I do not wish to cast aspersions on that dear and fervent community, but just to state facts.

All that is changed now, and everyone, including the pupils, uses the missal and has it explained to them. What I have said shows too, how differently the reading of *The Liturgical Year* affected the various members of the Community. Me it fired with enthusiasm, others it left dry and uninterested. As I listened, a new world of deep spiritual beauty opened out before me.

It must be remembered that I never met any nuns but the Ursulines; that I knew nothing about other religious orders, knew absolutely nothing of active and contemplative orders. But now it began to dawn on me that the Church had a life all her own, that there were orders of monks and nuns who lived that life with her, who partook of the life-giving food she gave them in her daily Liturgy, whose chief work was to chant the praises of God, the Divine Office, the *Opus Dei*. As a Benedictine, my friend, Miss O'Callaghan, now Sister M. Constance, was one of these favoured souls. Now I began to envy her! Why had I not known? Why had I not known of the rich stories of Holy Church, and made them mine? The answer was simple:- I had not inquired.

It was some years before this took definite shape in my mind, which always moves slowly, but take shape it did and I had to own that my soul felt starved, and that I needed stronger food. With my usual reticence, I kept this to myself, and tried to adapt to my own case what I had heard in sermons or read in books about similar experiences: - 'This is probably a temptation; the devil experimenting on my pride, which always ambitions the highest and the best. I will shake off this discomfort when it assails me, as I should shake off sparks falling on my clothes. I will not let myself think about the matter'.

Somewhere about the summer of 1912 there was a political crisis in Belgium, in which the Catholic votes were threatened with a small minority, so powerful had the Liberal and anti-clerical party become in a short time. Should the Liberals win the elections, all religious orders would be suppressed, as they had been in France a few years previously.

One day about this time I was walking slowly round the garden, reading, and praying now and again, and some thought in my book impressed me. Perhaps the old tempta-tion assailed me again; at any rate, this thought came to me, clear and decisive: - 'I will never risk losing my vocation by asking to enter a Contemplative order, unless some great upheaval should occur which threatened to suppress or secularize us, and I shall take that as a sign from God that I may ask for a change'. I mention this because, in the course of events, this resolution played an important part.

The elections were held, and the Catholic party gained a considerable majority, so the danger of suppression was over, and life went on as before. 'To do the will of God is sanctity', I said to myself. His will is for me to remain here.

Then came the momentous year of the Great War, 1914. One day at the end of July I was reading a German magazine with some dear German girls who had been confided to my special care, and there before us was the account of the assassination at Serajevo. They looked at me in dismay, but I did not take such a serious view of the situation, nor did I for several days. 'These continentals get excited about nothing', I thought. And when I saw the children crying because their brothers had been called up, and when I saw two or three nuns ashy pale because the tocsin had been rung in the old parish church, I still thought it was much ado about nothing. I hung my head, humiliated, when I saw my mistake and found that the war had actually begun. With bewildering rapidity the enemy advanced, and Liége fell. Immediately, our extensive school premises were commandeered, and offices and chaplains and stretcher-bearers were sleeping in the dormitories. The poor Tommies, not even uniformed, slept on straw in the children's large playroom and in the cool corridors. How we ached for them all!

I have already referred to the dear German girls of whom I had charge. Their father's bank had failed, so they were obliged to qualify themselves to earn their living. I had found a very nice post for one of them with my dear friend, Miss O'Callaghan, now Sister M.Constance. For years I had not

written to her, except once when my dear father died, R.I.P.
While a novice I cut off all correspondence, except the home
letters. Perhaps this was foolish, but the intention was good.
It was such a pleasure to hear from her again, and to place my
little German protégée under her care. The war, however,
frustrated our plans. My little charge return to Germany, and
was married soon afterwards. When the war broke out, Sister
M. Constance used to write for news, and in her answers to
my letters, I learned that her Community had prepared
quarters for a Community of Carmelite refugees, and were so
disappointed to hear they had gone else where, and not to
Princethorpe. I remembered this when our turn came to take
refuge, and it was the Princethorpe address I gave to Reverend
Mother on that last dreadful morning, thinking she might
offer this Princethorpe refuge to a Community of
Redemptoristines taking refuge in our convent. They,
however, went to Holland with Canon Boone, and God
regarded my sacrifice by letting us go to Princethorpe instead.

Chapter 6

The story of our flight from Lierre and our subsequent arrival in that haven of peace - St. Mary's Priory, Princethorpe, I recorded at the request of my superiors, and this later appeared in *The Tablet* of 17 October 1914, and I think I cannot do better than reproduce it here.

THE URSULINES' FAREWELL TO LIERRE

The crisis came so suddenly that it seemed, as it were, to hold up one's ordinary powers of thought and action. It is true we knew that the community of our Mother House at Thildonck (which is on conquered territory), had been dispersed, whither, no one could say. Yet, at Lierre, one felt so secure, and looking back, our confidence seems almost unaccountable, but I can only tell you of the matter just as it happened.

Certainly, the grim realities of the struggle were vividly present to us; twenty wounded men lay in one of the day-school halls, which had been converted into an ambulance; thirty more, with their officers, were regularly billeted with us, sleeping in one of the children's dormitories; whilst another party of the rank and file, varying from three hundred to four hundred, occupied the Lecture and Study halls of the boarding schools, lying on straw as best they could manage. Then there were twenty infirm women refugees, accompanied by some religious, and these were soon followed by odd groups of women and children seeking temporary shelter, as we were forbidden to keep them beyond a limited time. Yet, it was not until Monday, 28 September, that our feeling of security received its first blow.

That afternoon we received between twenty and thirty old, infirm men, scarcely able to walk, in the charge of some kind Religious, whilst at sunset, twenty infirm members of the Navre Ursuline Community arrived. Hitherto, the Superior had been as confident as we ourselves, but now she judged it necessary to send away these more helpless ones, who could not be moved quickly. They were accompanied by forty-six Redemptoristines, whom they had received three weeks previously from Malines - one aged eighty being brought in a hand-cart - and also by a family consisting of father, mother and eight little ones, the eldest aged nine. With this sad party, came the significant news that shells were already flying over the convent at Navre.

It was not easy to supply for all these fresh guests with our already taxed resources, but we were able to manage. All the available cells and dormitories were soon lined with weary, outstretched forms. We retired to rest, some of our sisters lying on the floor, and extinguished the dim, ghostly light which was the utmost permitted in the town.

At midnight a bell sounded. The rest of the Navre community, a hundred and thirty in number, had been forced into sudden flight, and now, worn out with terrors and fatigue from the long tramp, were appealing to us for help. As if our Reverend Mother would not give them her very heart! She threw open her doors gladly enough, but alas! there was little hospitality to bestow. Still, they were thankful to lie down where they could, their heads resting on the pitiful little bundles which held their sole worldly possessions.

But what was this burden in the arms of one of them? A movement brought to my view a lovely little face - fit model for an artist's Christ-Child - and I saw a wee girl of perhaps two and a half years, seemingly of gentle extraction.

The Navre Sisters had found her, alone and wounded, lying on the road. Now a bullet had been extracted from the tiny thigh, and she was all smiles for her new friend, and turning bright, sweet eyes on all around. Who, whence, was she? Who can tell? Poor little living drop in the tide of innocent sufferers - a tide which has swelled during these past weeks into a mighty ocean, surging with uplifted voice before the throne of Him who claims, by Divine right, to requite its claim.

But it was only when all gathered for Mass that one realised the outcome of those past twenty-four hours. What a sight it was! No order of place was possible in the crowded chapel; soldiers touched shoulders with Religious in various habits; children, stricken men and women, there they all were, intent for the moment on one only Strength and Consolation - flocking to receive the Bread of the Strong. As I rose to go forward, my eyes fell on a group at the Communion rail. This has two steps leading up to it, which proved an obstacle to the small legs of two of yesterday's refugees, and their father was assisting the mites to descend. I cannot tell you why, but that simple incident seemed to pierce my heart. I do not think I had really cried before, but now I went to receive Our Lord with tears which rained down unheeded. But then, He too was gazing on that strangely filled choir of ours - and He understood.

An hour or so later, two of us were busy at our appointed task in the top dormitory, making soldiers' beds, when suddenly a loud cannonade burst upon our ears. We had become quite accustomed to the distant roar, but this was different, it sounded quite close. My companion, forgetful of our usual regulations, ran to the window, and seeing a gardener under the window, she asked him what was happening. He answered that the forts were opening fire.

A few minutes later we heard a strange, whistling, rushing noise over the house, something like a rocket being let off. You have heard about that shell! Yes, the papers told how it tore its way into the hospital, working frightful havoc, and killing a large number of the wounded. So our turn had come! At any moment we might be "across the bourne" which now seemed so near.

Yet no one appeared to be afraid; everyone was hurrying about on some hasty errand as we went downstairs. 'Where are you going?' I asked one of my sisters. 'Don't you know? We are to pack, two blankets and two changes if you can manage it. Each one will take her own bundle'.

Our Reverend Mother was standing in the hall. The expression on her face was indescribable, but she was giving orders with calmness and precision, directing the departure of our refugee guests. The Redemptoristines were going to Holland.

I drew from my pocket a piece of paper on which, a short time before, I had scribbled the address of a Benedictine Convent in England. At the end of Mass, the idea had flashed forcibly upon me that perhaps we might soon be homeless wanderers. And a friend's letter some days previously has told of these English nuns, who were ready and eager to receive their suffering sisters. Should I tell Reverend Mother so that she might use the address for some of those already in need? But then, what if we -? However, you see, I had just received Our Lord, and I handed the scrap of paper to our Superior. 'Read it, please, dear Reverend Mother,' I said; and then seeing her look of reproach at my interruption, I added, quickly, 'it might help you'. I remember this because these were my last words with her.

Upstairs, the dormitories presented a strange scene. How busy, how calm every one was!

'Have you a bit of string?'
'Do you think that this knot will hold?'
'Let me make this go in better for you.'
'Poor Sister! Look at her bundle!'

Yes, even then we had to smile at some of our ungainly packages, as the Sisters moved away with their burdens, some tied up at the four corners, and slung over their arms. It did not take long - perhaps half an hour - but who could take count of moments? Then we stood together in the Community room, and Reverend Mother spoke. She said that the Navre Superior had taken charge of us, as her own children, but she and her Community, being already "packed", had been obliged to go on to the station. All were to go, except eight and herself. These had been chosen by Canon Boone, who happily had come from Navre, so that we went in holy obedience, and this would help us. Those remaining ones would stay as long as possible, in the hope of retaining the house. Then she gave us her blessing. There was no time for an individual farewell. 'Go, go', she ended, and thus we left her.

A party of solders waited outside and took our bundles for us. How thoughtful and kind they were, these brave, simple men! One of our nuns, a Jubilarian of five years' standing, was wheeled in a chair which had been charitably lent to us. So we reached the station; but the Navre Community had already been sent to Antwerp; no delay could be permitted. But now, no more refugees could go to that town; we must go to Bruges. We pleaded and expostulated, and an officer came to our aid, so that at last we were crowded into a train. Now, surely, all was well, we should find our Navre friends at Antwerp. What a fine station it is! But when we arrived it was packed with anxious crowds, soldiers keeping strict charge over all.

On all sides we heard one word: 'England'. 'Does this train go to England, please?' asked a wan-faced peasant girl beside me. Yes, England was the one spot in all the world which spoke to these desolated ones of help, safety, life, even, if not happiness. But we could not leave the train yet. First, some wounded men had to be passed out. I saw one of them, but I could not look again. At last it was our turn, and you may imagine how we held our breath to hear the reply to our question as to the Navre Community. 'Yes, those nuns are in another part of the station, but you cannot possible go there', we were told. Orders were orders, they were to go to Bruges, we must stay where we were. In vain we implored to be allowed to pass, it was useless. At least an officer once more took pity on us, he managed to get us into a less crowded part of the station, and allowed us to send messages to some friends in the town. So we sat down on our bundles, said our Office, and waited. The Navre Community had been sent off - somewhere - and we were helpless, homeless, but not hopeless, for we knew how wonderful our Lord is.

Then it was that I spoke to the senior nun in charge, Mére Seraphine, about Princethorpe, the English convent. She told me to wire there at once, but this was more easily said than done. It meant a big expense, but besides this, all sorts of formalities were necessary, even a photograph, and I had none of these. By this time, friends from the town were coming to us, bringing food, and one of these sent off the wire for us. What a message it was! I had only one thought - to let the

Benedictines know our dire need. It seemed useless to ask for a reply, as we should be on the boat by the time they received my appeal, so I just said: - 'convent shelled, we come'.

Scarcely had this wire gone when I was seized with misgivings which soon were to increase into a positive agony, for, see my position. I was now proposing to my Community that we should make our way to an unknown country, in a destitute condition, in the mere hope of finding some utter strangers able and willing to receive us. At last our friendly officer obtained permission for us to leave the station, and we were received for the night by the Little Sisters of the Poor. They were very kind and gave us what places they could. Some of us even found beds, and others rested on mattresses, laid on the floor. The good Sisters could not give us food, being obliged to provide their aged charges with the alms bestowed, but our friends still kept us supplied with all necessities, more, indeed, than we should have had at home.

Meanwhile, we had appealed at the bureau for free tickets, knowing that these had been granted to others in similar plight.

'What order?' asked the official.

'Ursuline!'

'No tickets for you, then. That Order is rich'.

Rich! Well might we look at each other! But again Providence came to our assistance. Some of our 'Old Girls' begged in the town for us, and next day, once more we set out, this time with money for our tickets, only to meet with another crushing obstacle: 'Room on the boat only for starving peasants, none for you'. This was the judgment, and we quite agreed, but oh! it was a torturing suspense. What would become of us? The following day we could bear the uncertainty no longer, and decided to send a second wire to

Princethorpe, this time asking for a reply. As a matter of fact, the nuns there had already sent an answer to my first message, hoping to find us somehow, but we never got it. Thus Friday came, and we were still helpless. Then suddenly, someone called for me. 'A wire! a wire!' It was from Princethorpe, a reply to my second message. The next instant I was waving it amongst my Sisters. 'See they are waiting for us, delighted to have us'. Ah! how that happy word 'Delighted' was echoed from one to another, for even nuns do not find it easy to beg hospitality, you see.

It seemed that God gave us new hope before each fresh disappointment. Our way seemed clear now - at any rate, for the moment - when the order came that we were forbidden to leave the country.

On that Saturday, I sat down and began a letter to my Benedictine friend, telling her it seemed that Our Lord wanted us to stay and face, perhaps, the worst. The letter was never finished, for my acting superior suddenly came upon me. 'You and Mère V. are to leave at once in a boat for British subjects only', she said. Hitherto we had refused this plan, which had been previously proposed by the Council. Now there was no alternative; we were told to go. But the separation was only to be for a short time. Kindness in official quarters had been at work for us, and the rest of the Community hoped to follow us the next day. Meanwhile, we two were given permission to seek shelter at the house of my brother, who lived near London. It was a terrible rough crossing. At least I heard that we were at the mouth of the Thames: we had not been drowned in spite of my preparation for death!

What kindness met us as we landed! A number of people were busy disturbing milk and food; we were able to join in the good work for an hour or so before making our way further. Finally, we arrived at our destination, and proceeded to rouse my brother's house, for no one was yet astir at that very early hour. That was well for us, as we were not anxious for spectators to see our sorry appearance. But a real English welcome awaited us, and, though torn with anxiety as to the welfare of our Community, you may guess with what feeling of gratitude we went to visit Our Lord in a neighbouring church later on that day.

The evening brought a wire just as we were retiring to rest, for which we had not even dared to hope. Our Sisters had landed at Folkestone, and might be at Victoria even before we could get there. But their train was an hour late, so my good, kind brother won the race, and thanks to his untold kindness, we soon had the whole party - worn out, but full of intense relief - on their way in motor buses chartered by him to Euston. Numbers of people recognised our plight as we drove along; hats were waved to us, and many cheers raised for France and Belgium. Despite the midnight hour, we were advised to push on to Rugby. In any case, it was impossible to communicate with our Benedictine friends until morning. We spent the rest of that night in the Rugby waiting room, and how shall I tell of the overflowing kindness which was poured upon us there? The station was full of soldiers; many of these gallant fellows came and actually knelt before us, kissing our hands, and simply burning to do us service. The Community had been joined at Antwerp by a refugee family of two ladies and five little boys. One of these had a small Belgian flag. This was an object of real devotion to the 'Tommies' who knelt or sat, fondling the children. 'Don't be afraid; we'll never let that be trampled on,' they said, 'we are going out there tomorrow'. A gentleman offered me some coffee. I did not want it myself, but asked to hand it on. He mistook this for an act of unselfishness, and in less time than it takes to tell, soldiers were besieging us with cups of coffee. God keep and reward those brave, kind hearts!

At the first opportunity we wired to Princethorpe of our arrival, the first possible intimation of the fact. Even as the nuns there received our wire, we reached the little wayside station three miles from the convent. Tidings of us spread quickly, and every vehicle in the neighbouring village was gladly placed at our disposal. Such a woebegone crowd it was! Their faces looked sad enough, but I knew their hearts were still sadder. The wrench from home and country, the uncertainty of the fate of dear ones left behind, the dread of meeting unknown friends in a foreign country, the tragic circumstances which had so suddenly transformed the victims at the shrine of Holy Poverty into destitute beggars, so soiled, so weary, so thoroughly undone - all this was constantly wringing my heart with a mighty pain. But here is the monastery! And here the guesthouse! How beautiful everything around is, and how happy must be the inmates of such an ideal home.

Will they spurn us for our soiled and abject appearance? Do they realize how utterly destitute we are...? Foolish heart, wherefore dost thou doubt? The door is scarcely opened when all our sad misgivings die a shame-faced death in the warmth of the reception given us by the Daughters of St. Benedict. Such pity! Such divine compassion! Who amongst us will ever forget the thrill of that first moment? It was not mere charity they gave us - it was love; and if any spot on earth possessed and used the power of binding up torn hearts, it was Princethorpe. My poor Sisters at once forgot their misery and their exile; their kind friends had been longing to receive them into their beautiful home, and now there was no possible doubt they had done far more, they had taken them into the depths of their noble hearts. The monastery bell rings for Benediction. We take our places in the beautiful church, so thankful to kneel once more at the foot of the altar. "*Come unto me and rest*". Yes, that was just what we wanted to do.

The organ breathes out a few notes, and then began the divinest song I ever heard in my life. Soft and low, solemn and stately, yet oh! how sweetly the voices rose and fell with the sympathetic strains of the organ. This heavenly harmony brings a message to my soul which hushes for ever the tumult that had been raging within it. The din of dread war, the cries of heart-broken refugees, the roar of winds and tempestuous waves, the strange noises of our mighty metropolis, even the dead weight of responsibility - all die away. God has drawn my bruised heart right into His, and there it rests and heals.

Chapter 7

The joy of meeting Sister M. Constance after fourteen long years was one of the great joys of my life. It was too deep for words, so unexpected, so wonderful. Everything was wonderful at Princethorpe. The more I saw, the more I marvelled, and yet I marvelled more at what I could not see, but could feel, and that was the spirit of the place, the people, the sanctity, and the sanctity of the Benedictine life.

Never, never shall I forget the Benediction of that first evening. The Benedictines were already in their stalls at the lower end of their beautiful church - Pugin's church - when the sixty-two Ursulines filed in and took their places in the children's benches, in front of the altar. As I knelt there before the tabernacle, and listened to that singing in which the soul seemed to speak through the voice, the strange experience of Braslau was repeated. I have never had it since. An overwhelming conviction came to me that this monastic life was the life I had longed for. From the depths of my soul came the cry: - 'O God let this life be mine; let me live and die here'.

It was astonishing how quickly our refugee life was organised by these clever Benedictines. The Archbishop had given permission for us to live with them in the enclosure, and so we worked and lived together. Our recreations was spent apart, and after the first day or two, we took our meals in their library, which became our refectory. Some of us taught in the school, some helped in the linen and habit rooms, others in the scriptorium, while our dear lay sisters helped in the kitchen and laundry. Mother M. Scholastica, the sister of Archbishop Mostyn, gave us wonderful lessons in plainchant. So the days sped on while we basked in the sunshine of the Christ-like loving kindness showered on us at every moment, and in every form.

It was only a few weeks after our arrival that my dear sister and her fiancé came from Edinburgh to see me. They had been on the point of coming to Lierre when the war broke out. It was delightful to see them and have long talks with them. Several of our "Old Girls" came too, and I had seen my dear friend, Mary, at my brother's house the day before we came to Princethorpe. Many of the "Old Girls" sent most useful and welcome gifts, and many were the letters of sympathy received. One of these was from one of my earliest pupils, whom I taught in my old school, Dorothy McIntyre, a dear shy little child she was then, with lovely dimpled cheeks and big questioning eyes, now she is the mother of three children! She writes to me still at regular intervals, and sends me valued presents of clothing. God bless her!

As the days passed, my longing to be a Benedictine increased, and at last I resolved to speak of it to my friend, Sr. M. Constance. She took a serious view of the matter, but was afraid to give me encouragement. I saw a great deal of her, because, fortunately for me, her room (the Head Mistress's room) was next to the room she had given up to be our Community room. It was an immense relief to be able to talk things over with her. She had a boundless store of common sense and of kindness, and I can never thank her sufficiently of all she did for me, and for the Community.

To our great surprise we learned that Canon Boone had not remained long in Holland with the Redemptoristines, but had brought them to England, and now was coming to see us. 'This is my chance', I told myself, 'I must speak to him about my desire to be a Benedictine'. It required a tremendous effort to do so, especially as I knew his opinion on the matter was of vital importance. He listened attentively, and then asked if I had ever entertained the thought of being a Benedictine before coming to Princethorpe. My prompt, 'Yes, definitely', impressed him, and he told me to pray, and to wait for the 'acceptable time', when God might grant my desire. I was much encouraged by this, and now resolved to write two letters, one to my dear old Novice Mistress, Mère Seraphine, who was in charge of the Community, and one to Dom Desimpel, a Flemish monk of Downside Abbey, who often came for confessions for those who did not speak English. It was only a year or two ago, when clearing out, that I burnt my letter to Mère Seraphine. I am so sorry now. In it I traced as best I could the growth of my longing for the contemplative life. I reminded her of my early days in the novitiate when I asked for liturgical books, especially the missal. I reminded her, too, of the strange fear that overcame me on the eve of my profession, when in order to comfort me, she took me in her arms, and tried to reassure me. And I think I finished by asking her to allow me to apply for entrance in a Benedictine Abbey. That letter I carried about with me nearly two years, waiting for a propitious moment.

My letter to Dom Desimpel I kept, also the answer he received from his friend, Dom J.C. Fowler, O.S.B., whom he consulted on the matter. In my letter to Dom Desimpel, dated 11 November 1914, and which I still have in my possession, I tried to set down the hopes of my being called to the Benedictine life - and my fears. I acquainted him with my history, and I now quote: -

I was received into the church in 1899 at the Ursuline Convent, Lierre, where I had recently been a grown up pupil. I was then twenty-three. It was the first convent I had really known, and I was naturally (perhaps not supernaturally) drawn to it. I never once questioned as to which convent I should enter, nor did I ever consult my confessor. You see, I was naturally of an independent character, accustomed to carve out my life for myself. Of course, this was a mistake. So I entered at Lierre in 1900, determined to be a thorough religious. I was in earnest, and before God, I can say that during all these fourteen years, I have not lost sight of my ideal, and, so far as was possible to a soul who seemed to be in her wrong sphere, I served God wholeheartedly with an ever increasing consciousness of the poor quality of my service, but with an increasing desire to make it more worthy of him. But I was not happy. Once, as a Novice, I told my Novice Mistress this. She explained to me that God requires some souls to bur (as it were, after having received it) the grace of their vocation by suffering and by serving Him in the dark.

In spite of my disappointment in the religious life, I rarely, if ever, lost my peace of soul. I looked upon the disappointment as a probable temptation, and as I rarely spoke of temptations, I never spoke of this. I never took root in my Community. Year by year I felt stranger. I tried not to show this, only I felt I was getting more and more self-repressed. I used to remember St. Paul's words:- "I die daily".

It was painful to find that I had to try to feel an interest in the convent and its work, to find myself lacking in *espirt de corps*, and oh! how often I have reproached myself for my want of attachment to my community! God, who knows the secrets of all hearts, knows my efforts, but I could not love and be enthusiastic about that which I could no longer admire.

Of course, I never let this be noticed. I really tried hard to *me faire tout a tous*. This went on until our sudden flight from Lierre when it was bombarded. Even when the shells were flying overhead, I made time to go to the chapel to say goodbye to it - I knew I should never see it again. I kissed the ground and thanked Our Lord for all he had given me there. As to the rest, I left the convent without a pang for myself. I suffered for my Sisters, seeing their grief, and I loathed myself for my own personal indifference. Perhaps Our Lord is less severe in his judgment of me than I was of myself....Now I was always afraid of confronting the question: - "Have I really mistaken my vocation?" Because it seemed to be one of those temptations to be shaken off as one shakes off sparks from a garment. But once, at least, I let myself consider the question, and that was two years ago, at the time of those critical elections in Belgium, when religious were threatened with secularisation. Then I seriously thought: - "Supposing I have to go away, I wonder if God will let me at last devote my life to the *Opus Dei*"? The elections were held and we remained.

I explained how we, as a community, had found ourselves here at Princethorpe, and how in this I again saw the hand of God guiding me. I was anxious for his advice and guidance, and willing to accept God's will:

During these last few weeks, I have been through a bitter conflict, but I can say quietly and calmly:- "Do what Thou wilt with me, O my God, but only let me be always thine".

All that I have said will explain my longing for the Benedictine life.

Here are my fears: - (1). Is the devil making a dupe of me by unsettling me in one vocation, in the hope of making me lose the religious vocation altogether? (2). I am naturally of an artistic temperament, in my former life I had to crush it continually. Here I revel at the way Art and its attendants are pressed into the service of God. But I recognise, too, that these things, even the *Opus Dei* itself, though they lead to God, are not God Himself. Am I being carried away by them?

Can the Ursuline become a Benedictine? Will you find out and tell me, please Father? If Rome forbids it, then of course, the matter is ended, and God's will is clear. . . .

I am sure, dear Reverend Father, that you will pray for me. This is a crisis in my life. Pray that the 'powers of darkness' may have no influence on me.

In his reply Dom Desimpel enclosed the letter he had received from his friend, Dom Fowler, and which I now give here:

Belmont Priory,
Hereford.
6th December 1914

Dear Father Desimpel,

I have read carefully the letter of your client, and also your own letter. You have done right, I believe, to discourage her attitude of unrest. It does not do to accede to a change at once, and the rebuff has the advantage of testing her humility. At the same time, I venture to say that the written statement of her case, as put by herself, is very strong, and is also quite calm. This obliges one to consider it fairly. As to Canon Law, a passing from one order or congregation to another used to be allowed very rarely to nuns, but I cannot say whether the law be relaxed now. The transfer cannot be made, however, without application to the Holy See. This application should show just cause, and stronger reasons would have to be given if the Superior of the order which a person leaves makes an objection.

I cannot say who would be the right person to present the petition. It is quite true that every individual may have access to the Holy See, but there is always a right order of procedure, and it is not clear to me whether it should be through the Superiors of the order, or through the diocesan. This point, however, may be settled later.

In the case of this nun, I cannot help thinking that the desire is genuine, and not an illusion. Her present profession never seems to have been *ex corda*, though it was *voluntaria*, and for her genuine advance in perfection. It may be well for her to obtain permission to follow her desire. She will have to make sure that the order she desires will receive her. But let not your client hurry. She must pray, and she must act simply. It may be awkward to go from the Ursulines to the Benedictines when she is in the house of the latter. If prompt action be necessary, let your client be quite straight about it and carry out her desire in due order.

If action be decided on soon, you must try to advise her of the right order of procedure. These matters are always troublesome. We must do our best that what is right may be done.

Yours very sincerely,
J.C. Fowler, O.S.B.

How grateful I was to God for this answer, and how high my hopes soared! I cannot remember now whether it was I who spoke to Reverend Mother Prioress, asking her if she would receive me, or whether it was Father Desimpel who did it for me. In any case, I was actually accepted by her and her council. Then it was found impossible to carry out St. Benedict's injunction that no abbot may receive a member of another community without first having the permission of that person's abbot. Communication with my poor Reverend Mother who had collapsed from the strain of war, was out of the question, and therefore, I must be refused. This was indeed a crushing blow. Dom Desimpel was so sorry for me, and suggested I should try some other Benedictine Monastery. Should he write to the Nuns of Ypres, an Irish community of Benedictines who had lived in Flanders for nearly two hundred years, until the war had driven them out, and now they were settling in Ireland and opening a school there. He wrote for me, but the answer was a refusal. A few months later, however, a letter came to him from the Mother Prioress of Ypres, who was acting for the aged Lady Abbess, suggesting that I should ask to be lent to them for a year, to help inaugurate their school. During that time, they would be able to test my vocation, and I should be able to test them. But how to get the permission? It must be given by Bishop De Wachter who had charge of all the Belgian Refugee Communities. Dom Desimpel said he would see the Bishop if need be, and meanwhile, he would ask the Prioress to write to Mère Seraphine begging the loan of me for a year.

A day or two later, Mère Seraphine called me to her. 'I have two letters here asking for your help. One is from Reverend Mother of a convent in Cambridge, who wants you for some Belgian refugees. The other is from the Mother Prioress of the Irish Benedictines of Ypres, who wants you to go to her in Ireland, to help her begin her school. I am puzzled by this letter. Why should she want you?' Then fixing me, she said:- 'Is there any truth in what our nuns tell me about your desire to be a Benedictine?' The bomb had fallen at last! Quite calmly I answered, 'Yes. Will you read this letter when you have time?'

She did read it, and calling me to her again, assured me that every word I had said was true. 'What am I to do?', she said, 'which of these two petitions for your help shall I answer?' 'Ma Mère,' I said, 'it is not for me to choose. I only wish to obey, and in doing so, to do the will of God.'

She looked surprised, and touched. After a pause, she said, 'your answer makes me believe God is directing you, and has special designs for you. I will not stand in your way. But to show you are really detached from your own will, go to Cambridge, and not to the Benedictines.' I bowed assent. I knew it was God's Holy Will for me, that alone gave me strength to go. How could I leave Princethorpe? Every fibre of my being was fast rooted in it, and to leave it tore my heart to pieces. Never had I loved a place as I loved Princethorpe. In it I had found new life. In it I had seen unrolled (no longer in book form, but in reality) the whole splendour of the Liturgical epochs, each one bringing its own special grace and blessing. The great events of our Saviour's life were no longer beautiful stories from the Gospel; they were not dead, but living realities.

But the agony of being thus uprooted, revealed something to me - that I loved it and my friend too much. While being borne heavenward by their magnetic influence, I had allowed myself to become earthbound. On the Feast of Our Lady of

Sorrows, Mère Seraphine and I were travelling through the beautiful quiet Midlands to Cambridge. I think my work among the refugees was successful, and the three months passed rapidly. All the time, I was upheld by the thought that God would do something for me: 'I have loved thee with an everlasting love, therefore I have drawn thee.'

Meanwhile, kind Dom Desimpel, unknown to me had gone to London to put my case before Bishop De Wachter, who expressed the desire to see me before giving his decision. It was providential that I was no longer needed in Cambridge, and I was, therefore, free to rejoin Mère Seraphine and the few remaining Ursulines (several had been allowed to return to Belgium) at a house she had rented at Beckenham, London. As many of the nuns were earning money by teaching refugees, she was able to do this, and so relieve the dear Princethorpe Community of the expense they had so generously borne for so long. With her I went to see Bishop De Wachter, with the result that I was allowed to go to the Benedictines in Ireland, on the terms proposed by them. It was wonderful news, and I rejoiced that at last my hour had come.

Mère Seraphine was all goodness, and Dom Desimpel sent me a present of money (given to him for Christmas) to defray my expenses. My dear brother and his wife came to see me and say goodbye. The former had paid me a visit at Cambridge, and I had shown him Dom Fowler's letter. He seemed glad that I was getting that which I had so long desired, and we had such a happy afternoon together. I have not seen him since then, and that was just twenty-eight years ago. My dear sister was in Edinburgh, and could not come so far in the bitter, frosty weather, and I was not sorry, for goodbyes are so painful.

Mère Seraphine accompanied me to Euston. She had been so good to me, and had helped me in every possible way; she even assured me that, should I fail in my new life, she would receive me back again with open arms. I knew she felt my departure very keenly, but she was bright and cheerful until the train began to move slowly out of the station. Then her face changed. It became grey with an expression of a suddenly realized loss. I have never forgotten it. She continued to write to me until her death. She told me she had kept my long communion veil for herself, and has passed hers to a new comer. Dear soul! R.I.P.

Macmine Castle, Co. Wexford.

PHOTO © IBAR CARTY

Chapter 8

When I arrived in Ireland I found it snowbound, as England had been. The Lady Abbess received me most kindly, and I felt at home. In my heart there was great joy and peace; the outcome of perfect surrender. This time there had been no self-seeking. I had come to strangers in a strange country. This time it was God alone I sought, and not God plus self-gratification. All attachments had been snapped, and as I walked alone, so light of heart, I sang to myself, '*Thou hast burst my bonds asunder.*'

I lived with the Community, but did not go to the Divine Office. I continued the Ursuline prayers and the Little Office, and worked hard in the school and in the garden, and often in the fields, "tinning" the turnips, which I discovered, meant thinning them. The Community was very poor, and great poverty was the order of the day.

After a few months, the Lady Abbess told me she and the Community were to receive me if I still wanted to join them. Of course I did, and at once I applied to the Holy See for permission to enter the great venerable Benedictine Order. After waiting for several months, the rescript came from Rome allowing me to enter the novitiate.

Someone told me that I had been labelled "Benedictine" at birth, and another remarked that the Order of St. Benedict had given me a great welcome, for I had received his holy habit on the feast of our holy mother St. Scholastica, and had made my holy profession on his own feast! Can anyone imagine my joy at being a Benedictine at last! It was unspeakable. I can still see myself walking along a pretty path with purple crocuses peeping up all around me, reading for the first time as a Benedictine, the Holy Rule. How reverently I opened it! It was mine at last. He was my father at last, and I his child. How I hung on his opening words: - 'Hearken, O my son, to the precepts of Thy Master, and incline the ear of thy heart, willingly receive and faithfully fulfil the admonition of thy loving Father'. Loving Father! Yes, that was it! And Oh! the pride and joy of receiving the holy habit, the Benedictine Breviary, and my own place in the monastic choir! There to take my part in the *Laus perennis* - the never-ending praise, which day and night, the Benedictines are privileged to chant to their Lord and King, praying too for their brethren in the world who pray not. Surely no woman could have a higher vocation than this! And to think it is mine! All unworthy though I am of it. When this sense of unworthiness tends to oppress me, I think of dear St.Paul, and with him say: - 'I will glory in my infirmity that the power of Christ may dwell in me'.

As I still had my Ursuline vows, I was exempted from the temporary vows, and admitted at once to perpetual vows, on 21 March 1919, feast of our holy Father, St. Benedict. It was a day of days. With what fervour I sang the Benedictine *Suscipe*! How proud I was when the Bishop placed the little, gold ring on my finger, and gave me the monastic cowl! And when I received our dear Lord, how I thanked and thanked and thanked! This holy profession was all light, so unlike the other which was dark.

Deo Gratias (Thanks be to God), I had chosen for my motto. It was engraved inside my little ring, but more deeply on my heart. I love my motto more and more as life advances, and gratitude increases. Often when going up and down the stairs, I say '*Deo*' on one step, and '*Gratias*' on the next. May I continue saying it until the end and at the end!

Peace and joy deepen as the end draws near. Far off it cannot be, for I have just completed my span of life - three score years and ten. The last twenty-seven wonderful years, I have spent as a Benedictine in Kylemore Abbey - this little earthly Paradise in the heart of the Connemara mountains, to which we came from Macmine in 1920. It is one of the beauty spots of the earth. Remote from the world, its solitude and almost unearthly beauty make it an ideal Benedictine home. Hardly have you crossed the threshold, when you are at once rapt in contemplation of the beauties surrounding you, and drawn by them to their loving Creator. The eternal hills all around you, the mountain streams and torrents, the river and lakes, and the ravishing song of the birds, preach silent sermons, of which one never tires.

Surely, the royal poet, David, must have been dreaming of Kylemore when he penned his immortal song: -

> O all ye works of the Lord, bless ye the Lord!
> Praise Him and magnify Him for ever.
> O ye sun and moon, bless ye the Lord!
> O ye stars of heaven, bless ye the Lord!
> O ye showers and dew, bless ye the Lord!
> O ye night and day, bless ye the Lord!
> O ye mountains and hills, bless ye the Lord!
> O ye fowls of the air, bless ye the Lord!
> O ye sons of men, bless ye the Lord!
> Praise him and magnify Him for ever!

Dame Magdalen finishes her story on her 70th birthday. She lived for a further six years and died on 14 March 1952, after a stroke, though she suffered greatly from shingles for the last couple of years of her life.

I first met Dame Magdalen in 1938, when I came to school at Kylemore as a very junior, junior. At that time there was a junior school as well as the secondary school in Scoil Áine. All the juniors were boarders and we saw quite a lot of Dame Magdalen. She supervised some of our meals, some study time and was with us quite often at recreation on Saturday and Sunday afternoons. She also taught us to recite poetry, mostly choral recitation. Many of the poems she selected were rather above our heads - she was a great admirer of Francis Thompson and Sir Walter Scott. By the time I met her, her sight was very poor and she could no longer read, so that she loved one of us children to read to her. For me this was a great pleasure and we both enjoyed children's classics such as *A Flat Iron For A Farthing*, *Misunderstood* and *Pride and Prejudice*. While one read to her, she would knit, just plain stitches that she could do without seeing.

She had been Headmistress of Scoil Áine for a while, and had the most gentle way of correcting one, which was far more effective than a scolding. As you can see from her writing, she was a wonderful story-teller, and at the beginning of each school year we would ask her to tell us the story of Kylemore and Mitchell Henry. I think she romanticised the tale slightly, because some of her 'history' was not quite accurate, but she certainly instilled in me a love of Kylemore, its history and the people connected with it.

She was guest-mistress when Kylemore had a guesthouse, and gave much time to looking after all the guests and visitors who came to the Abbey. But in spite of such distraction, she never missed the Divine Office or the liturgy, and having a lovely voice she was a great asset to the choir.

There was one occasion on which she unwittingly did a great service to the Republicans. It was soon after the nuns came to Kylemore, during the Troubles. Either the Auxiliaries or the Black and Tans came up to the Abbey and she went out to the terrace to talk to them. Seeing the machine guns, and feigning innocence, she asked what they were, and the soldiers said they would give her a demonstration, so they fired across the lake, thus warning every Republican for miles around of their presence.

To the best of my knowledge none of her contemporaries knew she had written this lovely account of her early life. Apparently she gave the manuscript to her friend, Cecile Allison, an ex-pupil from the school in Lierre (Lier), Belgium. It was Cecile's son, Anthony F Allison, who forwarded it to Kylemore many years later and for years it lay hidden in a back cupboard. When it was discovered in 2000 the Community was overjoyed and decided to publish it and give it the public airing it was so obviously written for.

Dame Magdalen was a gentle, cheerful person, a true Benedictine and it was a privilege to have known her.

Sr Benedict O'Beirne, O.S.B.
Archivist
Kylemore Abbey